If the dinosaurs came back

If the dinosaurs came back

Written and illustrated by
Bernard Most

Harcourt Brace & Company
San Diego   New York   London

Library of Congress Cataloging-in-Publication Data
Most, Bernard
   If the dinosaurs came back.
Summary: A young boy who wishes for the return of
dinosaurs imagines how useful they would be.
1. Dinosauria—Juvenile literature. I. Title.
QE862.D5M67   77-23911
ISBN 0-15-238023-X (pbk.)

Special Edition
for School Book Fairs
C D E

Printed in Hong Kong

More books by Bernard Most:

Happy Holidaysaurus!

Pets in Trumpets and Other
   Word-Play Riddles

A Dinosaur Named after Me

The Cow That Went OINK

The Littlest Dinosaurs

Dinosaur Cousins?

Whatever Happened to the Dinosaurs?

My Very Own Octopus

For Eric and especially for Glenn,
who wished the dinosaurs would come back

I like dinosaurs.
I think about them all the time.
I read about them.
I talk about them.
Oh, how I wish the dinosaurs
could come back!

If the dinosaurs came back,
they could carry my daddy to work and back.

If the dinosaurs came back,
we wouldn't need
any more lawn mowers.

If the dinosaurs came back, house painters wouldn't need any more ladders.

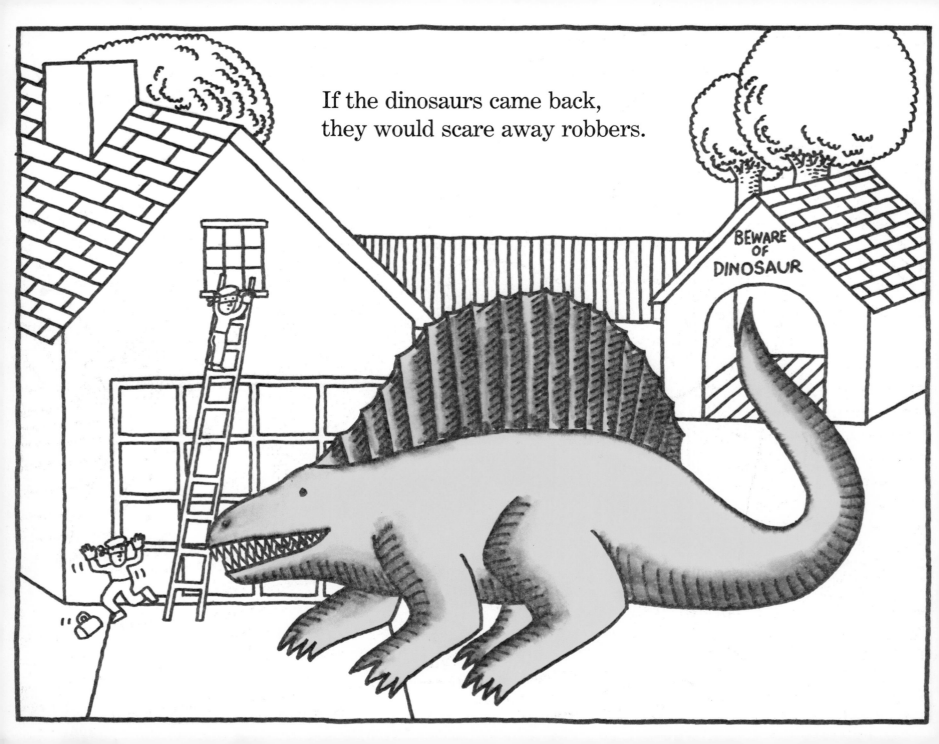

If the dinosaurs came back,
they would scare away robbers.

BEWARE
OF
DINOSAUR

If the dinosaurs came back,
they would make it easy for farmers
to plow their fields.

If the dinosaurs came back,
they could help lumberjacks chop down trees.

If the dinosaurs came back,
they could help fire fighters
put out fires.

If the dinosaurs came back, they could help build big skyscrapers.

If the dinosaurs came back,
they would make great ski slopes.

If the dinosaurs came back,
they could take swimmers
on rides at the beach.

If the dinosaurs came back,
they could rescue kites
stuck in very tall trees.

If the dinosaurs came back,
mountain climbers would
have new mountains to climb.

If the dinosaurs came back,
they could be a big help at the circus.

If the dinosaurs came back,
they could help librarians get books
from the top shelf.

If the dinosaurs came back, dentists would have plenty of teeth to work on.

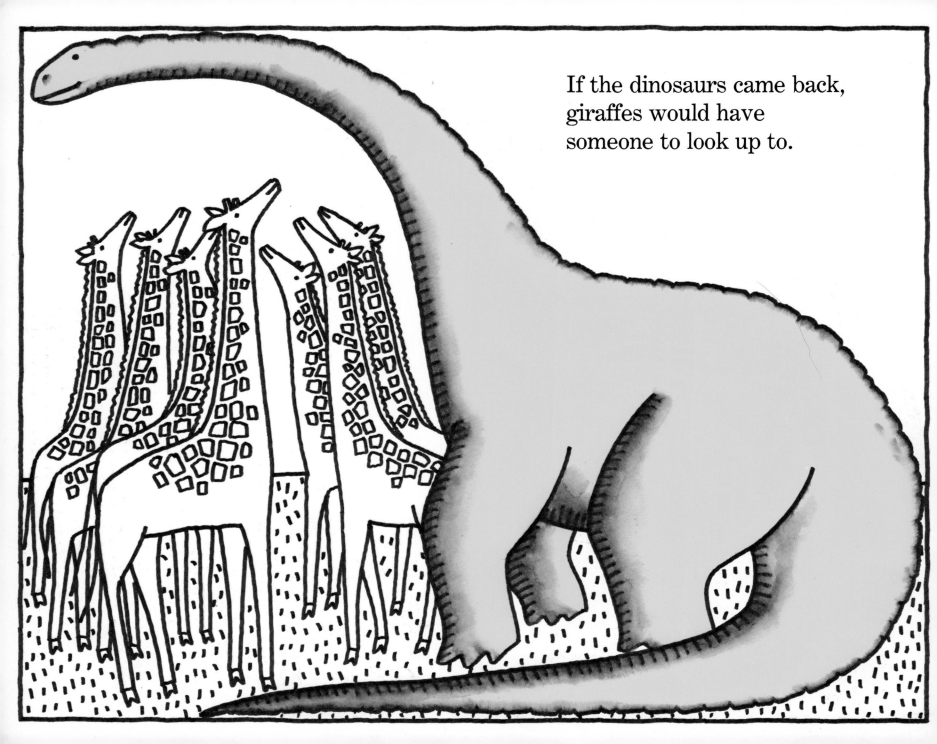

If the dinosaurs came back, giraffes would have someone to look up to.

If the dinosaurs came back,
they could push away rain clouds
so the sun would always shine.

But best of all...if the dinosaurs came back, they would make great pets for people who love dinosaurs.

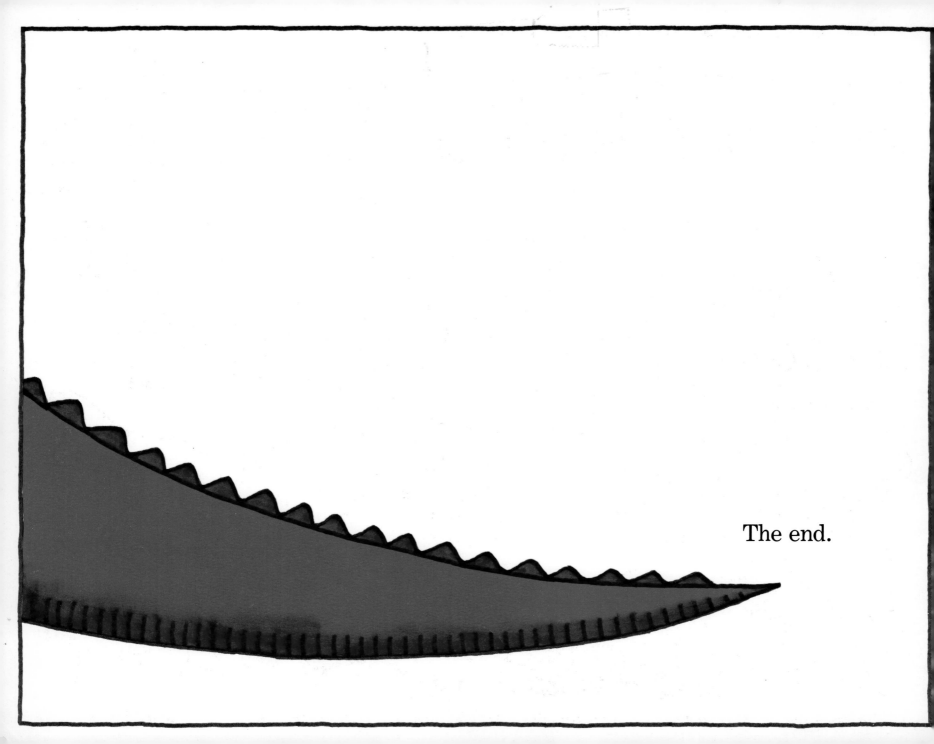

The end.

If the dinosaurs came back, this is what you would call them.

Diplodocus

Corythosaurus

Triceratops

Brontosaurus

Dimetrodon

Tyrannosaurus

Iguanodon

Ornithomimus

Plateosaurus

Allosaurus

Parasaurolophus

Trachodon

Plesiosaurus

Megalosaurus

Brachiosaurus

Stegosaurus

Hypselosaurus

Ceratosaurus

Coelophysis

Scelidosaurus

Camptosaurus

Protoceratops

Monoclonius

ABOUT THE BOOK

What would happen if the dinosaurs returned? Would they trample towns, smash automobiles, mash up people like asparagus? "No!" declares a little boy, who dreams of having a dinosaur of his own. Dinosaurs could help build skyscrapers and catch lost kites. They could push away rain clouds and plow farmers' fields. And giraffes would have someone to look up to. . . .

An imaginative and charming fantasy, Bernard Most's first picture book will enrapture dinosaur lovers everywhere.

ABOUT THE AUTHOR-ARTIST

Bernard Most grew up in New York City, where he graduated from the High School of Art and Design. He went on to attend Pratt Institute in Brooklyn, from which he received a Bachelor of Fine Arts degree. Mr. Most is the author of many books for children.

His son Glenn loved dinosaurs so much when he was eight years old that he wished they would come back. That gave Mr. Most the idea for this picture book, which was written to amuse Glenn and his younger brother, Eric.

Bernard Most lives with his wife and family in New York.